HOW TO MAKE MONEY BLOGGING

THE ULTIMATE GUIDE TO MONETIZING A BLOG WEBSITE

How To Make Money Blogging: The Ultimate Guide To Monetizing A Blog Website

Sarah Goldberg

Table of Contents

Chapter 1

Who Needs Money?

Chapter 2

Advertise Your Way to the Bank

Chapter 3

Affiliations DO Pay Off

Chapter 4

Guest Posts Do Make Money

Chapter 5

Sell Your Own Products and Services

Chapter 6

Write Anywhere and Anything

Chapter 7

Conclusion

Chapter 8

Resources & Further Reading

Chapter 1 - Who Needs Money?

Alternatively, perhaps I should ask who needs **extra** money. As the world struggles to claw its way out of the one of the worst recessions seen in years, people are finding it necessary to tighten their belts more than ever. Interest rates are at an all-time low, meaning that, while mortgage payments may be the lowest they have been in years, savings are sitting stagnant. Your money is going nowhere and there never seems to be enough of it to cover everything.

There are options. You could try to take on a second job, or even a third in some cases. However, some people are turning to the internet to try to earn some extra money. There are thousands of sites, all telling you how easy it is to earn money online, for just a few minutes of your time each day. Despite what you may read, it isn't very easy to make cash online unless you know the right way to do it. There are plenty of ideas out there, but not a lot of actionable plans to actually make you money.

One of the most popular methods for trying to earn money is through a blog. It sounds simple enough – you set up a blog site and start writing about a subject you love. But a word of warning - you can write to your heart's content; you can go on there every single day and update your blog with new information and stories but it won't make you any money. Why not?

Anybody can write a blog. Not everybody can make it work. That's the key – making your site work for you instead of you doing all the work and getting nothing in return. To make your blog work for you, you need to add to it – and I'm not just talking about adding more content.

The purpose of this eBook is to tell you how to make money from blogging. It's to show you no less than *5 different methods you can use* – all of them proven and all of them highly successful. This eBook is going to show you how you can turn your time and effort into money, **a potential goldmine** if you do it right.

Follow these methods and you will start to see money rolling in. You don't need to do them all at once. In fact, it is probably best if you don't – too much too soon will probably seem like too much effort and will have you exhausted. The trick is to start slow and build up your efforts and skill. Benefit from the knowledge of others, from learning how to turn a failure into profit and how to make your bank balance look quite a bit healthier!

Over the next 5 chapters, I am going to tell you, in detail, about each method: how it works and how to use it to its full advantage. I will tell you of the success stories, of people that have made money using each method and I will tell you how much money you can expect to earn in a month for each of the methods

Follow me as I lead you down the path to success.

Chapter 2 - Advertise Your Way to the Bank

Advertising can take many forms when it comes to making money. There are two steps to advertising – the first one is to concentrate on advertising your own blog. If you do not, the amount of traffic you get will be minimal and we all know that, in this business, traffic is money. Targeted traffic is worth even more. Let's assume though, for the purpose of this book, that you have plenty of traffic. People are visiting your blog everyday but you are not making a cent.

The second step, then, is to think about placing ads on your blog. There are loads of ways you can do this, the most popular method being Google AdSense. Google AdSense places advertisements on your website at no cost to you. All you have to do is choose the placement of the ads and the format in which they will be shown. The ads are directly related to the content of your blog and you get paid when someone clicks on an ad. Do not be fooled into thinking you can make a ton of money by asking your mate to sit there and click all day though – Google has built-in checks to ensure that clicks are only counted from an IP address once. You also cannot click on the ads yourself because you run the risk of being removed from the program. The best time to start Google AdSense is when your site is receiving at least 500 unique visitors per month and obviously, the more visitors, the more you will make!

Another way to make money through Google AdSense is to agree to have a Google Search box added to your site. Google is the largest search engine and giving people the option to search from within your site is a huge plus. Commissions are paid on a percentage of the advertising revenue gained by Google, determined by search terms. The potential is there to make huge sums of money via this method, especially if your site is generating a lot of traffic.

Banner ads are another option – if you have plenty of traffic you can sell advertising space to individuals or businesses. For this to be successful, you need to have a really great site, with at least 10,000 monthly visitors. You must also think very carefully about the placement for banner ads – you do not want them to take the eye off your own content but they must be visible as well. The most common places are across the top or down the sides to achieve that balance.

You may think that you cannot make any serious money just by placing advertisements on your site. In all truthfulness, some people will not even get one click or sell on spot. That is because their blog site is simply not attractive enough and does not bring in enough traffic so again, that 500 unique visitor/month minimum is key to making serious money with AdSense. As for the earnings, with Google AdSense you can expect to make anywhere up to around $5 per week with that 500 unique visitor/month target – not a vast amount to start with but as your traffic increases so will your earnings. However, you will see people claiming to have made thousands every month – it is possible if you have several highly successful, high traffic websites but I wouldn't be banking on making that much money when you just start out. Banner advertising is a different matter. You can sell banner ads for around $20 per slot per month so, let us say for example you sell four of them. That's $80 for one month. **Add that to your AdSense earnings and already you have made $100 in one month, just from advertising.** That's over $1000 you're making each year for doing nothing except posting a few ads on your site! Passive income at its best!

One success story that stands out is for the website www.askdavetaylor.com. The owner joined AdSense 10 years ago and, within 2 months was earning enough from the ads to pay his web-hosting bill. By the end of the third month he was able to pay his mortgage payment for that month. Since then, the amount of visitors to his site has increased and so have his earnings. He's a shining example of how to make a great income from passive strategies, and I'd recommend checking out his site for more on his story and how to succeed with these methods. As always, it takes time, some work, and patience, but just like Dave did, you too can generate significant passive income!

Chapter 3 - Affiliations DO Pay Off

One of the marketing techniques you hear about quite frequently is affiliate marketing. Not only is it one of the most popular forms of making some cash, it is also one of the easiest. With this type of marketing, you become a kind of partner to a business and you make your money by advertising their products or services. There are 3 ways that you can make money with affiliate marketing:

- Pay per Click – You get paid a certain amount according to the amount of clicks on the advertisement

- Pay per Sale – You will receive commission on any sale that comes from a referral via your blog site

- Pay per Lead – You will receive commission on ever new lead that subscribes to the business site by clicking on the ad on your site.

It really is very simple – all you need to do is sign up to a specific business, place a piece of code into your website and wait for your visitors to start clicking on the ads. Most affiliate sites are free to join as well. The best one to start off with is Amazon Associates. Amazon is a huge company, with thousands upon thousands of different product lines. In addition, they pay commission of up to 10%, depending on the quantity of the products you list on your site and the product type you're advertising.

The trick with affiliate marketing is to sign up with businesses that are related in some way to the content of your blog. Let's say you have a blog about pets. You would be looking for affiliate businesses such as pet stores, set supplies, animal feed, vets, etc. An easy way to start monetizing your site would be to review pet products that are for sale on Amazon and then add the affiliate link to your site. You're adding value to your readers (a quality review of a product) and if they buy the product, Amazon makes money and so do you! It does not matter what product it is, as long as it bears some relation to the service or product you are selling or the subject about which you are blogging. One important note is that there are specific guidelines that have been issued by the FTC which you must read in their entirety and you must post specific information on your site. Though not a comprehensive guide, you can get started reading about this here.

There are other great affiliate companies out there that compile affiliate links to a variety of companies. You sign up at one (or all three) of these companies and then can apply for a variety of affiliate links through companies like Apple, Vistaprint, Dropbox, ADT Home Security, and more! Here are three great affiliate companies:

1. Rakuten Linkshare

2. Share A Sale

3. Commission Junction

That said, do not go overboard with posting reviews and affiliate links all over your site. Getting the balance right is important but tricky. Too many ads on your blog site screams of desperation. Too many ads that shout "Buy it now!" will have the same effect. Do not forget, your job as an affiliate is not to sell – it is to provide value to your readers and make a commission secondarily.

The real question is, how much money can you earn through adopting affiliate marketing? Some affiliate links are extremely valuable—**even as much as $100 per sale!** That is not an easy question to answer – it obviously depends on your blog, how many visitors you have, how often they click through the ads and visit other sites. With a readership upwards of 500 unique visitors per month and if you post high quality reviews of products, its fairly easy to earn around $50 a week with this type of marketing. Obviously, the more visitors you have, the more click throughs to other sites and the more sales this generates, the more money you will earn on commissions.

There are some massive success stories to be read about. Earnings of $50,000 and upwards per year are not unheard of Obviously these stories are of bloggers who have a solid readership base and provide great quality to their readers. **Let's stick with just trying to earn that $50 per week for now, add that to your advertising revenue from Chapter 2 ($100 per month) and already you've made $300 in one month!**

Chapter 4 - Guest Posts Do Make Money

Having your own blog is great, especially when you can spend your time writing about things you love, things you have a great deal of knowledge about. However, that does not pay the bills does it? One great way to earn some extra cash as a blogger is to get into the field of guest posting. To be a guest poster there are several requisites:

- You must be very knowledgeable about the subject
- Your post must be completely original
- Your post must be on a subject that hasn't been beat to death
- If it is a popular topic don't give up if you have a completely fresh perspective on the subject
- You must have your own web or blog site

There are many sites that will pay quite a chunk of money for guest posts, some of them are offering upwards of $50 to $100 per post. Write four of those in a month and you are looking at anywhere between an extra $200 to $400 income, per month.

Here are three great sites that pay from $50 to $100 per post:

1. Read Learn Write
2. Your Biz Online
3. Be A Freelance Blogger

Be warned though, it's not an easy way of making money right from the outset; it takes practice to become a really great blog writer. Be prepared for rejections to start with. Sites that advertise for guest posters are very strict in their requirements. They will not give you an answer straightaway – you might find you are waiting anything from a day to a month before you get an accept or reject email.

Rejections are normally because the content is too weak or thin. The subject may be one that has been written about so many times, there is not anything new to say. On the other hand, perhaps you have filled your post with links – this is a strict no-no when it comes to guest posting. Some may allow you to put one link in but that's it. If the post is poorly written, i.e. poor grammar or spelling, it will be rejected. It is not their job to check it; it is yours and if it is not perfect, forget it.

That said, if you are highly knowledgeable about a specific subject the potential is there to earn some big bucks. When you are first starting out in the business of making money by blogging, you will not have much time for extras – you will be too busy maintaining and promoting your site and gaining your traffic. Once your site is ticking over nicely, then you can go on to allocate some time to other projects. Writing a guest post is not as easy as just churning out half a dozen articles. It cannot be just rehashed content. Therefore, it is perfectly fine to set your sights on just doing one or two a month to start with once your site is up and running.

Then, when you have more time on your hands and you have had a few posts accepted and published, you can start thinking about doing a few more. You can also add a link on your own blog site, directing your visitors to your new content and vice versa. This has the effect of building up your traffic and the other blog's traffic quite a bit as guest posting is an SEO "best practice".

You must also be on the ball – if your guest post is published and readers ask you questions or make comments, you must respond to them quickly. One thing that will put people off very quickly is being ignored.

We have already talked about money, about how you could, quite conceivably earn anything from $50 to several hundred dollars per month just by submitting successful guest posts. There really are no limits and there are no real success or failure stories to point to. Quite simply, you can earn as much as you want to earn by submitting guest posts. You could, if you were really successful, base your entire income around this one technique. Think about it – each 500-word post is worth $100 – perhaps it takes you an hour to write it – that is $100 per hour. If you could write five per day, 5 days of the week, that is 25 hours at $100 per hour –**that's $2500 per week**. Realistically speaking, if you can get half a dozen guest posts accepted in a month, you'd be doing well, and averaging $75 per post ($100 for 3 posts and $50 for 3 posts) you're at $450 per month. The real trick is learning how to write great blog posts in order to get them accepted and that's where the time and work lies. However, as with anything, practice makes perfect – keep working at it away and pretty soon, you will have an income to be proud of.

The tally now stands at $300 per month from advertising and affiliates plus $450 per month from guest posting and you're at $750 per month!

Chapter 5 – Sell Your Own Products and Services

If you are running a blog site for informational purposes, it will be something that you are passionate about, that you have knowledge about. Can you turn that into money? Yes, you can, in several ways.

To start with, you could write an eBook and sell it through your site. Do not rehash content that you have already written about for free – people will not pay for it. Instead, think of something that is related to our content that you have not talked about yet. Let's say, for example, that you run a blog site about cooking. You could write and sell an eBook that contains recipes that you have not yet divulged. Taking that one step further, you could also easily set up a membership site where people pay perhaps $10 per month for 5 new recipes delivered to their email inbox. These techniques are **powerful**. If you sell even 30 eBooks a month at $2.99 per book and earn a 70% commission (the Amazon standard for eBooks at that price) you're earning over $60 per month of passive income. Let's say that those people also have signed up for your membership site: That's $300 per month for that technique alone!

If you are blogging about SEO and marketing techniques, then think about making webinars which is tremendously easy via Google Hangouts. Google Hangouts allow you to host webinars on any topic you want and then these are saved to your YouTube channel. You can give a series of webinars on a variety of topics and give out great content in video format (which is very SEO-friendly!)

Alternatively, if you really are knowledgeable enough to consider yourself an expert, devise an entire online course. Take those webinars and expand the knowledge in each webinar. Give the first pieces of information away for free in the webinars then sell the rest as a course. Again, this can be easily accomplished via Google Hangouts, as you can make your longer videos that are a part of your course private, accessible only to certain people: the ones who have signed up for your course! You will be surprised how many people will sign up for something paid after receiving something of great value for free and many online courses are at least $50 to enroll. Think about that: 10 people sign up for a course and you're at $500 right there!

Got a product idea that will go with your blog? Having to keep stock means spending money – not just on the stock itself but on storage and then you have the hassle of postage and tracking. The simple answer is, let someone else do it for you. Someone like CafePress for example. They will take your idea, turn it into something personalized and sell it for you. You get a cut of the profits without having to lift too many fingers to do it. You will need a link on your blog site but that is not difficult and it is free. So, let's say that you have a branded T-shirt that you're selling on CafePress and you sell it for $23 on CafePress; they get $18 and you get $5. If you sell 50 T-shirts in a month, that's $250!

To be perfectly honest, there is no way you can put a monetary value on these techniques but they are certainly **powerful**. Remember, everything hinges on how much you can sell and for what price you sell it at. Remember this as well then: if you're selling a premium product, you can charge a premium price! So, let's say that you do an eBook and membership site and add that to the techniques in Chapters Two, Three, and Four. **That's $300 + $750 = $1050 per month, again without a huge time commitment or investment!** If you do an online course, you could easily earn $500 per month for that plus a branded item on Cafepress that earns you $250 per month. **If you employ all of these techniques, you're looking at $1050 + $500 + $250 per month. That's $1800 per month that you're earning without you having to do anything after setting it all up!**

Chapter 6 – Write Anywhere and Anything

Blogging is not just about writing your own blog. There are hundreds of websites that will pay you to write for them, although some will pay only small amounts. You can earn a reasonable amount of money doing this though and can write anything, from reviews to articles and other blog posts. Do not get this mixed up with Guest Posting – I have already covered that in an earlier chapter and this is very different. Although the principle is the same , they are different methods altogether.

Have a look at SponsoredReview.com. There, you can connect with advertisers, marketers and those in the SEO business and get paid to write reviews for them. Of course, if you are feeling flush, you can pay someone to write a review of your site, hopefully driving more traffic your way. However, that is not what this is about.

Another site that will pay you to blog is called CrowdContent.com. There, you can choose from a variety of work, all of which will have been requested and submit an article for approval. You start low on this site and work your way up but, if you are good at what you do, it will not take you long.

ContentBLVD.com is worth a look as well. Again, you get to look through a list of topics that articles are needed for certain blogs. If your article is accepted you'll get paid, if not, you could be asked to revise it and then resubmit it.

ReviewMe.com is a website that requires you to have your own blog or website. Once you have been approved, your blog will go onto the marketplace and you just wait for people to buy a review from you. You can earn anywhere from $20 - $200 per review with this site.

Fiverr.com is worth a look as well. Sell your writing services for $5 a time – for example, write an ad that says you will write an 800 word blog post for $5. If purchased and accepted, you will earn $4. A few of these each week soon adds up fast!

Squidoo.com is a great place to start if you want to get a bit of free advertising for your website. You can write pages, or lenses as they are known, and publish them. Ads are then placed onto your lense, similar to AdSense, related to the subject of your lense. Write content related to your blog site, you can link back to it, and you can also place affiliate links on there, especially if you are a member of Amazon Associates. You will receive approximately 50% of all revenue gained from the ads and links.

To be honest, I could go on and list site after site that will pay you to blog. The internet is littered with them but, unfortunately, not all of them are genuine. The ones listed here will definitely pay out for your blog posts provided your work is accepted.

When it comes to success stories for writing blog posts for other people, there are plenty of them. Some people have managed to earn enough money to give up their day jobs, while others have earned enough just to give them a better lifestyle, or pay a few bills. Depending on your style and tone of writing you can earn as little or as much as you want. In addition, if your writing is approved at some of the more prestigious sites, the more you write the higher up the rankings you go. And that only means one thing – more money.

Let us talk money for a minute. It is very difficult to place a monetary value on this type of work. You can as little as $2 per article up to $40-50. Guest posting will pay you better but the acceptance guidelines are much stricter. But, in terms of ease, this method of writing is a very easy way to generate money from your blog! With enough writing on a variety of sites above, you can easily earn a few hundred dollars per month. **Add that to the previous methods above, which can generate around $1800 per month for you, you're now earning over $2000 per month utilizing the easy methods above that** *don't take any technical knowledge*!

Chapter 7 - Conclusion

In order to make money blogging, you need:

- Enthusiasm
- Professional approach
- A passion for what you are doing
- Time to produce great content for a specific subject area
- Effort and dedication

Dedication and passion are two of the most important factors for success in any field and with blogging it is no different. Those factors lead to great blogs, which then leads to the ability to make money with your blog. Remember to focus in on why you want to make money blogging. Perhaps you are just looking to earn a little extra money and you have the skills to write your way into profit. Perhaps you already have a blog and you have decided it is time to monetize it.

Whatever your reason, you must believe in it and, if you decide to follow any of these tips or methods, you must be prepared to work at it. Each and every one of these methods requires work and time, more so in the beginning as all of these methods do require investments of time up front in order to set yourself up for success. Eventually, your hard work will pay off and you will be able to spend less time working on your blog and more time enjoying the profits you are making!

Resources And For Further Reading

Online Video Tutorials

These educational programs are hosted on the website Udemy, an easy-to-use educational platform. Each course is highly recommended with excellent reviews on Udemy and they've helped a ton of people learn the "next steps" to monetize their blog to start making money from their websites! You'll no doubt find additional ways to monetize your blog in these courses, and all of the authors have been **extremely** successful in earning additional income from their blogs.

How To Make Money Online Selling and Spend No Money Upfront

Course Description:

Learn How I Made an EXTRA $24,000 a Year Selling Online and Spent No Money Upfront For Inventory
Step by Step Guide
You know the phrase "You need money to make money" Well I wanted to prove that wrong. This course will teach you the actionable steps you can take to make money online by spending no money upfront.
About Matt Bernstein
Hi, my name is Matt Bernstein and I've been selling online since 2006 and I've SOLD over $750,000 DOLLARS in total. On January 31st 2012 I started Sports Pulse and I made my FIRST SALE 2 WEEKS LATER. SALES to date as of 12/1/2013 have been OVER $525,000.00.
$0 Upfront Costs on Inventory
You'll learn how to gain access to ANY product at WHOLESALE PRICES. You'll be able to LIST their inventory and when you make a SALE they'll SHIP your order. You NEVER need to keep an INVENTORY. You only buy the customers

order AFTER you make a sale. You make a PROFIT when you sell your items at RETAIL PRICES - wholesale prices = MONEY YOU KEEP!

Bloggers Creed: The Fastest Way To Earn Income From Blogging

Course Description:

Bloggers Creed is a powerful series of videos which will take you inside the world of becoming a pro blogger. We use a trademark system of creating "Blog Assets™." They are unheard of within the industry and will shake the current bloggers culture! These blog assets, also called "Harvest Blogs™" are used to generate sales using a small number of fans and low traffic. This is a completely new approach to running or starting a blogging business. This is for new and advanced bloggers.
Above all else, our videos are transparent, void of hype and contain real-life examples. We'll take you on the inside showing how full-time income was generated from new start-up blogs. Join bestselling author <u>Ansel Gough</u> and our community in launching or building your own blog and Blog Assets™ using the methodology which is Bloggers Creed.

Blogging Success Program

Course Description:

" I would definitely recommend this course to anyone **who wants to create a top blog and hit one million pageviews quickly**. The value you get is worth many times more than the price you pay!" ~ Alyssa Choong, Blogging Success Course Participant
"I've read many articles on blogging over the years and I have never found anything that matches what you will learn in this course. If you are serious about

having a successful blog, **you need this course**." ~ Marsha Roberts, Blogging Success Course Participant

"The Blogging Success Program was beyond all my expectations. After finishing the last module, I worked on my blog **for 5 hours straight** because I was so filled with ideas, energy and optimism!" ~ Roxi Staton, Blogging Success Course Participant

Blogging Success Program is my intensive six-module blogging video course sharing my best blogging success strategies growing my blog (Personal Excellence - http://personalexcellence.co) **from zero visitors to one of the leading personal development blogs online today with over a million pageviews a month: all in under three years**!

Besides my professional experience growing PE rapidly in just three years, my content and lessons come from over 10 years of web development and experience creating and running over a dozen websites in different genres.

Monetizing Programs

Google AdSense

Amazon Associates

Rakuten Linkshare

Fiverr.com

SponsoredReview.com

ReviewMe.com

ContentBLVD.com

CrowdContent.com

Squidoo.com

Share A Sale

Commission Junction

Read Learn Write

Your Biz Online

Be A Freelance Blogger

CafePress

Helpful Websites

Below are five links to websites that can help you in your quest to make money blogging:

http://bloggingwithamy.com/can-you-really-make-money-with-google-adsense/

http://www.problogger.net/make-money-blogging/

http://myclownworld.blogspot.com/2013/06/make-money-onlinewhy-affiliate.html

http://how-to-make-money-blogging-online.com/

http://christianpf.com/how-to-make-money-with-a-blog/

Books

For delving further into the world of monetizing blogs, these books provide helpful information:

How To Create Your Own Website & Earn Passive Online Income Easily - A Step By Step Guide to Building a Profitable WordPress Website! By Neil Saibhreas

Sell It Online 2: How to Make Money with Your Own Website, Blog, Kindle Book, or by Coaching &Training by Nick Vulich

Your First $1000 - How to Start an Online Business that Actually Makes Money by Steve Scott

How To Create A Website With Wordpress And Start A Profitable Online Business by Ming Jong Tey

A Pirate's Treasure Map - An idiot's guide to making money online by Robert Harding

Disclaimer

All attempts have been made to verify the information contained in this book but the author and publisher do not bear any responsibility for errors or omissions. Any perceived negative connotation of any individual, group, or company is purely unintentional. Furthermore, this book is intended as entertainment only and as such, any and all responsibility for actions taken upon reading this book lies with the reader alone and not with the author or publisher. This book is not intended as business advice and the reader alone holds sole responsibility for any consequences of any actions taken after reading this book; the author and publisher are not responsible for any monetary loss or gain that occurs as a result of following the methods in this book. Additionally, it is the reader's responsibility alone and not the author's or publisher's to ensure that all applicable laws and regulations for business practice are adhered to. Lastly, I sometimes utilize affiliate links in the content of this book and as such, if you make a purchase through these links, I will gain a small commission.